WELCOME TO ICE HOCKEY BIOGRAPHIES FOR KIDS

Paragon Publishing offers a wide selection of other sports biographies and quiz books, so be sure to check them out if you enjoy this one.

Paragon Publishing is a privately run publishing company which cares greatly about the accuracy of its content.

As many facts and figures in this book are subject to change, please email us at **ParagonPublishing23@gmail.com** if you notice any inaccuracies to help us keep our book as up-to-date and as accurate as possible.

Enjoy!

CONTENTS

INTRODUCTION

The National Hockey League (NHL) started in 1917 with four Canadian teams, all from the eastern part of Canada. The Boston Bruins were the first American team to join the league in the 1923–24 hockey season. In 2022, the United States now dominates the NHL with twenty-five teams versus Canada's seven.

Almost half of the players come from Canada, with the US making up just over one-quarter of the league and the remainder coming from other European countries. After all, hockey is Canada's national winter sport, and many kids are on ice skates by the time they are 3!

Imagine going to a new country at 18 years old, moving away from your family to join an NHL team, and not speaking a word of English. Think about the goalies in the early days who didn't even wear masks or other protective equipment and took puck slapshots to their faces! Imagine battling through broken bones and multiple surgeries and still rejoining your team in search of the big silver Stanley Cup, the ultimate hockey prize, each year. These are the hockey heroes we will celebrate.

These hockey legends were driven, passionate, and persistent in reaching their dreams of playing in the NHL. They were leaders and never gave up. We can all learn a lot from them.

WAYNE GRETZKY

Nickname	The Great One
Nationality	Canadian, American
Born	January 26, 1961
Position	Center
NHL Debut	1978
Teams	Edmonton Oilers, St. Louis Blues, New York Rangers

STANLEY CUPS
4

GOALS	ASSISTS
894	1963

BIOGRAPHY

On January 26, 1961, "The Great One" Wayne Gretzky was born in Brantford, Ontario, Canada. Gretzky first learned to skate before he turned three, and by the age of six, he played on a team of mostly 10-year-olds. By the time he was 10, he had scored 378 goals and 120 assists in a single season in Brantford's atom league.

Gretzky had already scored over 1,000 goals by the time he was 13. When he was 14, he played Junior B hockey with the Toronto Nationals on a team of mostly 20-year-olds.

As a 16-year-old in 1977, Gretzky was selected third overall by the Sault Sainte Marie Greyhounds of the Ontario Major Junior Hockey League draft. Gretzky first wore number 99 with this team. He had wanted number 9 worn by his hero Gordie Howe, but that number was already taken. In 1978, Gretzky signed with the Indianapolis Racers of the World Hockey Association before being traded to the Edmonton Oilers in the NHL. All this early practice helped him really develop his game, as he signed a 10-year contract with the Oilers by the age of 18.

In his first NHL year, 1979—80, Gretzky scored 51 goals and won his first Hart Memorial Trophy as the Most Valuable Player in the NHL, a streak that would continue

for eight years in a row. Not bad for a guy who was kind of skinny at 6 feet tall and 180 pounds! He was known for his passing and shooting accuracy and for always bringing out the best in his teammates.

Gretzky led the Oilers to four Stanley Cup titles before being traded to the Los Angeles Kings in 1988. He guided the Kings to the 1993 Stanley Cup Finals, scoring 15 goals and 25 assists in the playoff run before the Kings eventually lost to the Montreal Canadiens. Gretzky was traded to the St. Louis Blues for the 1995–96 season before joining the New York Rangers, where he finished his NHL career in 1999.

As rumor has it, he was superstitious about always drinking soda, water, and Gatorade between periods, and always in the same order. This ritual must have worked for him because when he retired, he held 61 NHL records and was the all-time leading scorer, with 2,857 points, 894 goals, and 1,963 assists. He joined the Hockey Hall of Fame in 1999, and his number 99 was retired across the entire league.

A year after his retirement, he became part-owner and head coach of the Phoenix Coyotes until 2009. In 2016, Gretzky returned to Edmonton to join the Oilers Entertainment Group as a minority partner. He left in 2021 to become an analyst for the NHL at Turner Sports.

In 2021, a rare 1979 Gretzky rookie trading card sold for $3.75 million. What a legend he was!

Jean Béliveau

Nickname	Le Gros Bill
Nationality	Canadian
Born	August 31, 1931
Position	Center
NHL Debut	1953
Teams	Montreal Canadiens

STANLEY CUPS
10

GOALS	ASSISTS
507	712

BIOGRAPHY

Jean was born on August 31, 1931, in Trois Rivières, Quebec, Canada and first learned to play hockey on his family's backyard ice rink. Béliveau's family moved to Victoriaville, Quebec when he was six, and he first played organized hockey with his school, L'Académie.

At the age of 15, while attending college at Victoriaville and playing for the Victoriaville Panthers, he was scouted by the Montreal Canadien's general manager. They wanted him to commit to a Canadiens contract should he turn professional, but he turned them down several times.

Before he turned pro, he was called up to play for the Canadiens twice in 1950 and 1951. He officially became a Montreal Canadien in 1953. He'd go on to play for them for eighteen seasons, becoming their team captain at age 30. His teammates described him as being a gracious, classy, and kind man who treated everyone with respect.

Béliveau quickly became one of the top players in the NHL. During his second full season, he was one of the top scorers, and in 1955–56, he led the NHL in goals and points. Unbelievably, he once scored three goals in 44 seconds!

He would play 1,125 regular season games, where he scored 507 goals. He won ten Stanley Cup Championships as a player and seven more as a Canadien's executive, which is still an NHL record.

Béliveau was the second player in league history to reach 1,000 points and the fourth to score 500 goals in a career. In 1972, Béliveau was inducted into the Hockey Hall of Fame.

Until his death, he was a proud ambassador of the Canadiens. Béliveau passed away on December 2, 2014. Two days later, the Montreal Canadiens started to wear a black patch with the number 4 on their uniforms in his honor. With Béliveau, the Canadiens achieved greatness.

MIKE BOSSY

Nickname	Boss
Nationality	Canadian
Born	January 22, 1957
Position	Right Wing
NHL Debut	1977-78
Teams	New York Islanders

STANLEY CUPS
4

GOALS	ASSISTS
573	553

BIOGRAPHY

As the fifth of ten kids, Mike Bossy was born on January 22, 1957, in Montreal, Quebec, Canada. Like so many other NHLers, he got his start by practicing on a backyard ice rink at his apartment building. Bossy played in the 1969 Quebec International Pee-Wee Hockey Tournament with a minor league team and started his junior career with Laval National at age 15.

Bossy was passed over by 12 teams in the 1977 NHL draft before being signed by the New York Islanders. In 1978, Bossy won the Calder Memorial Trophy as the top rookie in the NHL, setting a rookie record of 53 goals in a season. Bossy led the NHL in goals the following season with 69 and again in 1980—81 with 68 goals. He once scored nine hat tricks (three goals in a game) in one game!

Bossy would stay with the Islanders for his whole professional hockey career. He is still the only player to have four game-winning goals in a single playoff series, accomplishing that in the 1983 Conference Final. He had nine 50-goal seasons, tied with Alexander Ovechkin and Wayne Gretzky, and he holds the record for the most consecutive 50-goal seasons.

In 1991, he was inducted into the Hockey Hall of Fame. On March 3, 1992, the Islanders retired his number 22 jersey.

After retirement, Bossy became a radio broadcaster in 1993 and was part of a morning show in Montreal, staying with them until 1996.

He struggled to find a job with an NHL organization for nearly 15 years after he quit playing. He returned to the Islanders in 2006, working in sponsor and fan development. Bossy joined MSG Networks as a hockey analyst in 2014 and TVA Sports in 2015 as a color commentator.

Bossy developed lung cancer and passed away on April 15, 2022, at the age of 65. He will always be known for his slap shot and as one of the best shooters in NHL history.

RAY BOURQUE

Nickname	Bubba
Nationality	Canadian
Born	December 28, 1960
Position	Defenseman
NHL Debut	1979-80
Teams	Boston Bruins, Colorado Avalanche

STANLEY CUPS
1

GOALS	ASSISTS
410	1169

BIOGRAPHY

Ray Bourque, future defenseman extraordinaire, was born on December 28, 1960, in Saint-Laurent, Quebec, Canada. Bourque was raised speaking both English and French, even though he attended a French school.

He played in the Quebec Major Junior Hockey League for three years before he finally caught the NHL's attention in 1979. He was selected eighth overall by the Boston Bruins in the 1979 NHL Entry Draft. He won the Calder Memory Trophy for being NHL's top rookie in 1979–80. Amazingly, he'd stay with the Bruins for 21 seasons and held the titles of co-captain and captain.

In 2000, after requesting a trade, it was a sad day for Bruins fans when Bourque left to join the Colorado Avalanche. This proved a good move for him as he finally won his first Stanley Cup in 2001. In game 3 of the 2001 playoffs, at 40 years old, Bourque became the oldest NHL player to score a goal in a Stanley Cup Final!

Bourque was on the All-Star teams 19 times between 1980 and 2001. He has the record for most career goals, assists, and points by a defenseman in NHL history. He was the only defenseman to score 400 goals and was awarded the James Norris Memorial Trophy for the league's top defenseman five times. Bourque played on the 1998 Olympic team for Canada.

Bourque scored at least 20 goals in a season nine times and retired with 410 goals and 1,169 assists. He was also a bit superstitious, as he supposedly changed his skate laces before every game and even between every period. Over his 1,826 games, that was a lot of laces, but it obviously worked for him!

Fortunately, he retired a Stanley Cup Champion in 2001. He was inducted into the Hockey Hall of Fame in 2004, and his number 77 was retired by both the Bruins and the Avalanche. Bourque became one of only nine players to have his uniform number retired by multiple teams.

Bourque's two sons followed his NHL path. His oldest son Christopher made his debut in 2007 with the Washington Capitals and played for the Bruins in the 2012–13 season. Bourque's youngest son Ryan played for the New York Rangers in 2014–15.

Bourque will forever be known as one of the best defensemen in the NHL. He still lives with his wife in the Boston area, where he owns a restaurant and is involved in charitable work.

MARTIN BRODEUR

Nickname	Marty, Brody
Nationality	Canadian
Born	May 6, 1972
Position	Goalie
NHL Debut	1991-92
Teams	New Jersey Devils, St. Louis Blues

STANLEY CUPS
3

CAREER WINS	GOALS AGAINST AVERAGE
691	2.24

BIOGRAPHY

Martin Brodeur was born on May 6, 1972, in Montreal, Quebec, Canada. He started playing hockey as a forward and switched to becoming a goalie. During his teenage years, he studied different goalie techniques and was encouraged to use multiple methods. Brodeur played in the Quebec Major Junior League in 1989–90 before being drafted by the New Jersey Devils in 1990.

Brodeur won the Calder Memorial Trophy as the NHL's top rookie in 1991–92. He led the league in wins eight times over a nine-season period from 1997 through 2006, as the 2004–2005 season was canceled due to the NHL lockout. Brodeur won the Vezina Trophy for league's top goalie four times and finished second three other times.

Over 12 straight seasons, he won at least 30 games and holds the record with eight 40-win seasons. Brodeur retired with a record 691 wins, 125 shutouts, and 1,266 games played. He even scored three goals in his career, the most of any goalie in NHL history!

Brodeur would spend 21 seasons with the New Jersey Devils before accepting a one-year contract with the St. Louis Blues in 2014. In his 22 NHL seasons, Brodeur would win three Stanley Cups, all with the Devils.

He was inducted into the Hockey Hall of Fame in 2018. He played on Team Canada in the 2002 and 2010 Winter Olympics and won two gold medals.

Some of his success can be attributed to the techniques he learned at a goalie camp during his teens, where Vladislav Tretiak, a former Soviet goalie, taught him to adapt and innovate, resulting in Brodeur's unique style. He remained on his skates rather than initially adopting the more traditional butterfly style where goalies play from their knees. In his later career, he would use a hybrid style, adopting some butterfly elements. Before each game, Brodeur said he watched and studied the last game played against the team he was facing and always used a new stick.

He was much more skilled at handling the puck outside the crease than most goalies, acting as a third defenseman of sorts. In 2005, the NHL introduced the "Brodeur Rule," which changed where goalies were allowed to handle the puck outside of the crease.

Brodeur announced his retirement in 2015, leaving a legacy as one of the best NHL goalies ever. In 2016, he even got his own bronze statue, placed outside the Prudential Center in Newark, New Jersey! Brodeur currently works for the Devils as executive vice president of business development.

SIDNEY CROSBY

Nickname	Sid the Kid
Nationality	Canadian
Born	August 7, 1987
Position	Center
NHL Debut	2005-06
Teams	Pittsburgh Penguins

STANLEY CUPS
3

GOALS	ASSISTS
518	894

BIOGRAPHY

Halifax, Nova Scotia, Canada, was the birthplace of a future outstanding hockey player, Sidney Crosby, who was born there on August 7, 1987. He came from a hockey family of sorts as his dad played in the Quebec Major Junior Hockey League. By age two, Sidney started playing hockey in his basement and was on skates by age three.

From the age of 12 to 15, Crosby went to junior high in Halifax before he transferred to a boarding school in Minnesota in 2002–03 for their hockey program. He went on to play in the Quebec Major Junior Hockey League for two years, where he started to attract lots of media attention and began to fill his hockey résumé with awards. There was a lot of pressure on the guy, as many people were already comparing him to Wayne Gretzky!

In a truly exciting 2005 NHL Draft Lottery, the Pittsburgh Penguins scored when they picked up Crosby first overall in the picks. He made his debut that season, scoring 102 points on 39 goals and 63 assists, finishing 6th in the league. He finished second for the Calder Memorial Trophy as NHL Rookie of the Year. He led the league with 120 points in his second season in 2006–07, winning the Hart Memorial Trophy as MVP.

Crosby became captain of the Penguins the following season and led the team to a Stanley Cup Finals appearance, losing to the Detroit Red Wings after six games. The Penguins met the Red Wings again in the Stanley Cup Final the following season, but this time they came out on top after seven exciting games. Crosby gained the bragging rights of being the youngest captain in the history of the NHL to win the Stanley Cup.

Crosby led the NHL in goals for the first of two times in 2009–10, with 51 goals scored. He was out for most of the 2011–12 season with a concussion. Crosby rebounded in 2013–14, leading the league in scoring and winning the league MVP for the second time. He led the Penguins to two more Stanley Cup titles in 2016 and 2017, winning the playoff MVP both times. By the end of the 2017 season, he was already named one of the top 100 players in NHL history. He's led the Penguins to sixteen straight years of playoffs. It looks like his 5 p.m. pre-game peanut butter sandwich habit is really paying off!

On the international scene, Crosby has played for Team Canada many times. He scored a game-winning goal against the US in the 2010 Winter Olympics to win the gold medal. Crosby returned to the 2014 Winter Olympics, once again winning the gold medal.

As of 2021–22, Crosby has racked up some impressive stats, with 518 career goals, 894 assists, and 1,409 points. He still appears to have plenty left in the tank to climb well into the top ten before his career is over.

PHIL ESPOSITO

Nickname	Espo
Nationality	Canadian
Born	February 20, 1942
Position	Center
NHL Debut	1963-64
Teams	Chicago Black Hawks, Boston Bruins, New York Rangers

STANLEY CUPS
2

GOALS	ASSISTS
717	873

BIOGRAPHY

Phil Esposito, or "Espo" as he was known in hockey circles, was born on February 20, 1942, in Sault Sainte Marie, Ontario, Canada. He signed with the Chicago Black Hawks farm team in 1960 and played on the Sarnia Legionnaires Junior B team in the 1960–61 season. By 1964, he'd impressed enough to be called up to the Chicago Black Hawk's parent team for his NHL debut. (The Black Hawks would change their name to the Blackhawks in 1986.)

He would only spend three seasons with the Hawks before being traded to the Boston Bruins in 1967. He sure made an impression on his new team when he scored 100 points in the 1969 season, making him the first NHL player to do so. Esposito surpassed 60 goals in a season four times between 1970 and 1975 while with the Bruins, reaching a high of 76 goals in 1970–71. Esposito helped the Boston Bruins to win Stanley Cup titles in 1970 and 1972. His teammates considered him the glue that held the team together.

After spending the best years of his career with the Bruins, he was traded to the New York Rangers in November 1975 and named their captain. He'd score his 700th goal in his last season with New York before he retired in 1981.

Over an 18-season career playing for 3 NHL teams, Esposito scored 717 goals and 873 assists, with 1,590 points. Esposito won the Art Ross Trophy five times and the Hart Memorial Trophy twice. He probably attributed his success to his game-day habits. He always wore a black shirt under his jersey and taped his stick with black tape before every game.

Esposito was inducted into the Hockey Hall of Fame in 1984 and had his number 7 retired by the Boston Bruins on December 3, 1987.

After retiring, Esposito was head coach and general manager of the Rangers for two seasons before he and his younger brother founded the Tampa Bay Lightning in December 1990. Esposito was the team's president and general manager until 1998. There is a statue of him in front of Tampa Bay's Amalie Arena. That was sure to have made him smile as he said that starting that franchise was harder than playing in the NHL!

"Espo" was deservedly named one of the 100 Greatest NHL Players in History in 2017. He sadly died of cancer in 2021 at the age of 78.

GORDIE HOWE

Nickname	Mr. Hockey
Nationality	Canadian
Born	March 31, 1928
Position	Right Wing
NHL Debut	1946-47
Teams	Detroit Red Wings, Hartford Whalers

STANLEY CUPS
4

GOALS	ASSISTS
801	1049

BIOGRAPHY

Gordie Howe was born in the tiny farming town of Floral, Saskatchewan, Canada, on March 31, 1928. He had eight brothers and sisters, and money was tight in their house. The Howes moved to Saskatoon when Gordie was only nine days old. Howe started to skate by age four and began playing organized hockey at the age of eight. He was already six feet tall by his mid-teens. He played Bantam hockey in Saskatoon and was initially scouted by the New York Rangers, but he declined.

In 1944, he signed on to the Detroit Red Wings junior team before moving on to the Omaha Knights in the United States Hockey League in 1945. Howe finally made his NHL debut with the Red Wings in 1946, scoring 7 goals, 15 assists, and 22 points in 58 games.

He led the league in scoring from 1950 through 1954 and in 1956–57 and 1962–63. In his 25 seasons with the Red Wings, Howe won four Stanley Cup titles. He sure was no stranger to injuries during his hockey career. He broke multiple bones in his body and had more than 300 stitches. A fractured skull in 1950 couldn't even stop him!

Howe first retired from the Red Wings in 1971 when he was 43 and was inducted into the Hockey Hall of Fame in 1972. In quite a remarkable move, in 1973, he joined two of his sons in the newly formed World Hockey

Association (WHA). In 1979, the only four WHA teams were brought back under the NHL umbrella, and Gordie Howe found himself playing with the Hartford Whalers in the NHL for one last season in 1979–80, gaining the legacy of being the oldest man to play in a game in the NHL at age 52.

When he retired, Howe had 801 goals, 1,049 assists, and 1,850 points, which were all NHL records at the time. Howe was on the NHL All-Star team 23 times and held the record for most seasons played until 2021.

Famous for his scoring, strength, and longevity, Howe is the only player to have played in the NHL in five different decades. He played one shift for the Detroit Vipers of the International Hockey League in 1997, becoming the only player to play professionally for over six decades.

A bronze statue of Howe was unveiled in Joe Louis Arena, and another statue sits in Saskatoon at the corner of 20th Street and 1st Avenue. He was the first recipient of the NHL Lifetime Achievement Award, and in 2017, he was named one of 100 Greatest NHL Players.

Howe will even have a bridge spanning the Detroit River named after him, and he owns his own trademark, "Mr. Hockey." Howe died in 2016 at the age of 88.

DOUG HARVEY

Nickname	God
Nationality	Canadian
Born	December 19, 1924
Position	Defenseman
NHL Debut	1947-48
Teams	Montreal Canadiens, New York Rangers, Detroit Red Wings, St. Louis Blues

STANLEY CUPS
6

GOALS	ASSISTS
88	452

BIOGRAPHY

Canadian Doug Harvey was born on December 19, 1924, in Montreal, Quebec. He first played Canadian football for his high school team in 1939, and he was also a baseball player. Harvey also played for the school's hockey team, originally as a goaltender but later moved to center. Eventually, Harvey transitioned to defenseman, where he would play his entire professional career.

During World War II, Harvey joined the Royal Canadian Navy and spent the majority of his free time playing for the naval hockey team. It was at this time that Harvey gave up playing other sports to concentrate on a hockey career.

Harvey's professional hockey career began in 1945 with the Montreal Royals of the Quebec Senior Hockey League. He stayed with the Royals until 1947. After a season playing in the American Hockey League with the Buffalo Bisons, Harvey was off to the NHL and the Montreal Canadiens in 1947.

Harvey only scored 24 points in 90 games over his first two NHL seasons but earned the first of 11 consecutive All-Star honors starting in 1951—52. In those days, defensemen were expected to defend and not to score points. He played for the Canadiens through the 1960—61

season, winning five Stanley Cup titles. He was an excellent defenseman with amazing stickhandling abilities which led to the Canadiens becoming a high-scoring team. Harvey was selected for the NHL's First All-Star Team in 1951–52.

In 1961, he was traded to the New York Rangers likely in retaliation after he fought for players' salaries and rights and helped to set up a player's union. He'd stay there through the 1963–64 season until he asked to be released from his contract.

Harvey spent the next five years playing in the minor leagues in Canada and the US before he was called up to the NHL with the Detroit Red Wings for two games in 1967. Harvey joined the St. Louis Blues for the 1968 postseason and played one more season before retiring in 1969.

He was inducted into the Hockey Hall of Fame in 1973. Harvey had ongoing problems with alcohol and his mental health throughout his adult life. He landed a job working as a scout for the Canadiens in 1985. Harvey developed cirrhosis of the liver and died in December 1989 at the age of 65.

Harvey was named one of the 100 Greatest Players in NHL History in 2017. In addition to being remembered as one of the NHL's greatest defensemen, Harvey should be acknowledged for the players' union work he fought for that helped lay the path for today's players to be able to sign lucrative contracts with favorable contract terms.

BOBBY HULL

Nickname	The Golden Jet
Nationality	Canadian
Born	January 3, 1939
Position	Left wing
NHL Debut	1957-58
Teams	Chicago Black Hawks, Winnipeg Jets, Hartford Whalers

STANLEY CUPS
1

GOALS	ASSISTS
610	560

BIOGRAPHY

Bobby Hull, one of the all-time greatest NHL players, was born on January 3, 1939, in Pointe Anne, Ontario, Canada. He was on skates by the time he was three years old and practiced on a frozen bay on Lake Ontario. Bobby often played with his dad's amateur hockey league as a teen. He was scouted by the NHL by the time he was 12 and signed a future contract committing him to the Chicago Black Hawks.

He would continue to develop his hockey skills in the junior league circuit in Ontario, spending time with the Woodstock Warriors, the Galt Black Hawks, and the St. Catherines Teepees before getting called up to the Chicago Black Hawks for an exhibition game. He made a big impression by scoring two goals and proved he was ready for the big leagues. He made his NHL debut with the Chicago Black Hawks in 1957 when he was 18 years old, where he'd quickly earn the nickname "The Golden Jet" because of his blond hair, hard slapshot, and quick skating speed.

Proudly wearing his famous number 9 jersey and skating for the Black Hawks, Hull led the league in goals in 1959–60 for the first of seven times. He won the Hart Memorial Trophy as the NHL MVP in 1964–65 and 1965–66 and led the Black Hawks to the Stanley Cup title in 1961. He was the first player at the time to break the record of more than 50 goals scored in a season. He even played alongside his

brother Dennis for eight seasons in his Black Hawk days. Talk about sibling rivalry!

Money talks, and after 15 seasons with Chicago, Hull joined the newly formed World Hockey Association (WHA) for the Winnipeg Jets, signing a $1 million contract in 1972. He'd be an instant superstar in his seven seasons with the WHA and was instrumental in the Jets winning the Avco Cup (the equivalent of the Stanley Cup) in 1976 and 1978. His decision to join the WHA caused him to be excluded from 1972 Team Canada since only NHL team members were eligible. The Prime Minister of Canada even lobbied unsuccessfully to get the country's beloved player on the team!

After the 1978–79 season, the WHA was merged into the NHL after experiencing financial problems. In the 1979–1980 season, Hull would come out of retirement and play briefly for the Winnipeg Jets (who were now an NHL team) for only 18 games before he joined the Hartford Whalers for 9 games that same season. In September 1981, at age 42, Hull tried a comeback with the New York Rangers, which lasted all of five exhibition games. Hull retired with NHL stats of 1,063 games played, 610 goals, 560 assists, and 1,170 points. He scored 50 goals per season at least five times in his career.

In 1983, Hull joined his son Brett, also an NHL superstar, in making history as the only father-son duo to be elected to the Hockey Hall of Fame at the same time. The greatest left-winger of all time continued to be an ambassador for the renamed Chicago Blackhawks until 2021.

JAROMÍR JÁGR

Nickname	Jags
Nationality	Czech
Born	February 15, 1972
Position	Right wing
NHL Debut	1990-91
Teams	Pittsburgh Penguins, Washington Capitals, New York Rangers, Philadelphia Flyers, Dallas Stars, Boston Bruins, New Jersey Devils, Florida Panthers, Calgary Flames

STANLEY CUPS
2

GOALS	ASSISTS
766	1155

BIOGRAPHY

Jaromír Jágr, affectionately known as "Jags," was born on February 15, 1972, in Kladno, Czechoslovakia, where he lived on a farm with his family. Like so many other NHL stars, he started skating at the age of three.

By the time he was 15, he was playing at the highest level of hockey in Czechoslovakia for Poldi SONP Kladno. Jágr became the youngest player on the Czechoslovakia national team when he was 17 years old.

Prior to 1990, the only way a player born in Czechoslovakia could make it to the NHL was to defect. In 1990, once communism ended in his country, Jágr made history by being the first player to join a NHL team without needing to defect. He landed in Pittsburgh, not speaking a word of English but rocking a terrific mullet! In the NHL draft, he was fifth overall and selected by the Pittsburgh Penguins, where he quickly became a superstar.

Jágr was part of the Penguin's success in achieving Stanley Cup titles in both 1991 and 1992. He won the Art Ross Trophy for NHL scoring champion five times and four straight seasons from 1997–2001. He won the NHL MVP once and was runner-up four times. He was also named the league's most outstanding player by the NHL Players' Association three times.

Jágr was the face of the Penguins from 1990 through 2001, serving as the team captain beginning in 1997. In 2001, he joined the Washington Capitals for three seasons after signing the biggest NHL paycheck of the time.

In 2004, with the Capitals no longer being able to afford him, Jágr was traded to the New York Rangers and stayed there until 2008. His next move was across the pond to the Kontinental Hockey League, playing with Avangard Omsk until 2011. He landed back in the NHL for his final seasons. He played for one year with the Philadelphia Flyers, then split his 2012–13 season between the Dallas Stars and the Boston Bruins. Next up, he spent two years with the New Jersey Devils, three years with the Florida Panthers, and one year with the Calgary Flames to finish up his NHL career in 2017–2018 at age 46.

Jágr was the youngest player in the league when he entered and the oldest player when he last stepped on the ice in the NHL. He set a record in 2017 when he scored a hat trick, becoming the oldest player to do so. In 24 NHL seasons, Jágr played in 1,733 games, accumulating 766 goals, 1,155 assists, and 1,921 points. He is second all-time in points scored behind Wayne Gretzky. One record he didn't break was the number of NHL teams he played on!

Jágr will undoubtedly make the Hockey Hall of Fame on the first ballot when eligible. As of 2022, he lives in Czechoslovakia, and incredibly, at the age of 50, he still plays in the top Czech league.

GUY LAFLEUR

Nickname	The Flower, Le Demon Blond
Nationality	Canadian
Born	September 20, 1951
Position	Right wing
NHL Debut	1971 — 72
Teams	Montreal Canadiens, New York Rangers, Quebec Nordiques

STANLEY CUPS
5

GOALS	ASSISTS
560	793

BIOGRAPHY

Guy "the Flower" Lafleur was born in Thurso, Quebec, Canada, on September 20, 1951. He started playing hockey when he was five and practiced on the outdoor rink behind his house. At age 15, he was already a superstar in the Quebec Major Junior Hockey League, albeit a skinny one at 135 pounds.

Lafleur played for the Quebec Remparts until the 1971 NHL Amateur Draft took place. As one of the top prospects that year, he was selected by the Montreal Canadiens. At the age of 20, he'd accomplished his teenage dreams of playing with that team and proudly sported his number 10 blue, white, and red jersey.

While the first few years weren't exactly record-breaking for him, he was part of the Canadiens team to win the Stanley Cup in 1972–73. The team would go on to win four more Stanley Cups between 1976 and 1979, with Lafleur leading the team in scoring every year. He made NHL history by scoring 50 or more goals in six straight seasons and also had 50-plus goals and 100-plus points in six straight seasons. He led the NHL in points in 1976, 1977, and 1978, tying a club record of 60 goals in 1977–78.

In 1985, Lafleur retired for three years before rejoining the NHL in 1988 with the New York Rangers. He then spent two years with the Quebec Nordiques, completing

his two-decade NHL career in 1991.

Lafleur was an NHL All-Star for six consecutive seasons and led the league in games played four times. He retired after having played 1,126 games with 560 goals and 793 assists and joined the Hockey Hall of Fame elite in 1988.

He is one of only three players to have returned to the NHL after being inducted into the Hockey Hall of Fame. Lafleur had his number retired by the Canadiens on February 16, 1985. In 1998, Lafleur was ranked 11th on The Hockey News list of 100 Greatest Hockey Players and was named one of the 100 Greatest Hockey Players in 2017.

In 2019, Lafleur had open heart surgery, and he developed lung cancer in 2020. He passed away on April 22, 2022.

MARIO LEMIEUX

Nickname	The Magnificent One, Super Mario
Nationality	Canadian
Born	October 5, 1965
Position	Center
NHL Debut	1984-85
Teams	Pittsburgh Penguins

STANLEY CUPS

2

GOALS	ASSISTS
690	1033

BIOGRAPHY

On October 5, 1965, in Montreal, Quebec, Canada, "Super Mario" Lemieux first made his appearance in this world. He started playing hockey at the age of three inside his house before graduating to a homemade rink on the family's front lawn.

By an early age, Lemieux was dominating in the Quebec Major Junior Hockey league, playing for the Laval Voisins. He broke league records during the 1983–84 season by scoring 282 points in 70 games and adding 29 goals in 14 games during the playoffs. It didn't take long for the NHL scouts to come calling.

Lemieux struggled with his first days after signing with the Pittsburgh Penguins in 1984, picked first overall in the NHL Entry Draft that year. He was 19 years old, spoke little English, and suddenly had a $1 million, three-year contract in his hands. He scored his first goal during his first shift of his first game, then went on to lead the Penguins to consecutive Stanley Cups in 1991 and 1992. Lemieux led the league in scoring six times. He won the Hart Trophy for league MVP three times and the Conn Smythe Trophy as playoff MVP in 1991 and 1992.

He was sidelined by back issues in 1990–91 and was diagnosed with Hodgkin lymphoma in 1993. Lemieux was a true hero, persisting and battling his way back

from his health problems.

Lemieux was limited to 915 games out of a possible 1,430 regular season games but played his entire NHL career with Pittsburgh. At the time of his retirement, Lemieux was seventh all-time in career points with 690 goals and 1,033 assists. He holds the record for being the only NHL player to have 70+ powerplay points in a single season.

In 1999, Lemieux had one last powerplay with the team even though he was retired. With the Penguins in dire financial trouble, he and Ron Bourke, an American businessman, bought the Penguins franchise! Fenway Sports Group acquired the Penguins in late 2021, but Mario remains a part-owner.

Lemieux was inducted into the Hockey Hall of Fame in 1997. In 2004, he was inducted into Canada's Walk of Fame and was named one of the 100 Greatest NHL Players in 2017.

NICKLAS LIDSTRÖM

Nickname	Saint Nicklas
Nationality	Swedish
Born	April 28, 1970
Position	Defenseman
NHL Debut	1991-92
Teams	Detroit Red Wings

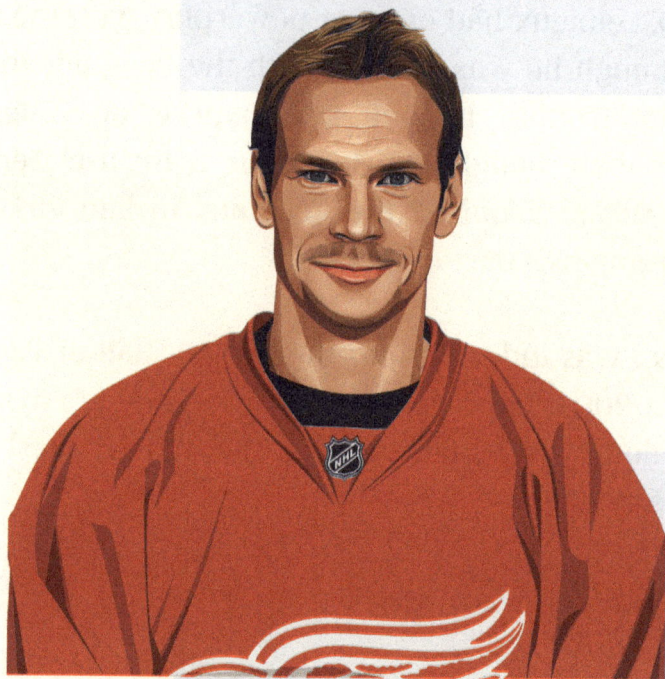

STANLEY CUPS

4

GOALS	ASSISTS
264	878

BIOGRAPHY

Nicklas Lidström was born on April 28, 1970, in Avesta, Sweden, two hours north of Stockholm. He got his start playing street hockey before he learned to skate. In his teenage years, he played with Skogsbo SK before playing with VIK Vasteras HK, scoring 12 goals and 30 assists in 103 games over three seasons.

The Detroit Red Wings drafted him 53rd overall in the 1989 NHL Draft third round. He debuted with the Red Wings in 1991-92 but played for Vasteras IK during the 1994-95 NHL lockout. As a rookie, Lidström finished second for NHL Rookie of the Year and was named to the 1992 NHL All-Rookie Team.

His teammates described him as always being unbelievably calm, polite, and one who never complained. He was able to hoist his first Stanley Cup in 1997 and was named captain in 2006.

During a career that spanned two decades, all with the Red Wings, Lidström won four Stanley Cup titles and one Conn Smythe Trophy as playoff MVP. In addition, he was an All-Star 12 times and top defenseman in the NHL seven times. Only two other players in league history won the Norris Trophy more than Lidström. He played in 263 playoff games and is also the only player in league history to play in the NHL playoffs in 20 consecutive

seasons. Lidström was the first player born and trained in Europe to be captain of a Stanley Cup champion team.

"Saint Nicklas" as he was nicknamed announced his retirement on May 31, 2012, at the age of 41. He retired as one of the best defensemen in NHL's history with 264 goals and 878 assists and is the record holder of the most games ever played by one player for one franchise (1,564).

A month after his retirement, he began scouting for the Red Wings. During the 2013-14 season, Lidström had his number 5 retired by the Red Wings. Lidström was inducted into the Hockey Hall of Fame in 2015 and was named one of the top 100 Greatest NHL Players.

Lidström released his autobiography in October 2019, titled *Nicklas Lidström: The Pursuit of Perfection.*

MARK MESSIER

Nickname	The Messiah, The Moose
Nationality	Canadian
Born	January 18, 1961
Position	Center
NHL Debut	1979-80
Teams	Edmonton Oilers, New York Rangers, Vancouver Canucks

STANLEY CUPS
6

GOALS	ASSISTS
694	1193

BIOGRAPHY

Mark Messier, also known as "The Messiah" and "The Moose" in the hockey world, was born on January 18, 1961, just outside of Edmonton, in St. Albert, Alberta, Canada.

Messier went to St. Francis Xavier High School in Edmonton and played in the Alberta Junior Hockey League and the major junior Western Hockey League. His next move was to the World Hockey Association, playing for the Indianapolis Racers and the Cincinnati Stingers between 1978 and 1979 before being selected by the Edmonton Oilers in the 1979 NHL Draft.

He developed into a brilliant center for the Oilers, scoring 35 goals in 150 games over his first two NHL seasons before breaking out with his only 50-goal season in 1981-82. By 1984, he'd land his first of five Stanley Cups with the Oilers and the Conn Smythe Trophy as MVP of the playoffs. Messier scored 20 or more goals in a season 17 times, four times surpassing 40 goals in a season.

Messier would stay with the Oilers until 1991 before joining the New York Rangers. He led the Rangers to their first Stanley Cup in 54 seasons and secured the bragging rights of being the only NHL player to have captained two Stanley Cup championship teams. Messier

also played three seasons with the Vancouver Canucks, scoring 52 goals before his last four seasons back with the Rangers. During a game between the Rangers and the Buffalo Sabres, Messier scored his final goal on March 31, 2004.

He announced his retirement at age 43. He played 1,756 games, finishing his career with 694 goals and 1,193 assists. On January 12, 2006, there couldn't have been a more fitting backdrop when Messier had his number 11 retired by the Rangers in a game against the Oilers in Edmonton. A little over a year later, Edmonton also retired his number, and he was inducted into the Hockey Hall of Fame on November 12, 2007.

At over 200 pounds, Messier was big, tough, and strong, but he was a passionate leader and team builder like no other. In fact, the NHL created the Mark Messier Leadership Award after Messier's retirement.

In 2017, he joined the ranks of the greatest, securing his name on the 100 Greatest NHL Players of all time.

STAN MIKITA

Nickname	Stosh
Nationality	Slovak
Born	May 20, 1940
Position	Center
NHL Debut	1958–59
Teams	Chicago Black Hawks

STANLEY CUPS	
1	

GOALS	ASSISTS
541	926

BIOGRAPHY

On May 20, 1940, Stan Mikita was born into humble beginnings in Sokolče, Slovak Republic, in a small farming community. His parents believed that Canada offered a better opportunity for him, so he moved to St. Catharines, Ontario in 1948 to live with his aunt and uncle when he was eight years old. Life wasn't easy for him, as he started Grade 3 in a brand-new country and not speaking a word of English.

Mikita's lead-up to the NHL began by playing with the Chicago Black Hawks farm team, the St. Catharines Teepees. He got called up by the parent team for the 1959–60 season and secured his only Stanley Cup by 1961.

During his full rookie season in 1959–60, Mikita had eight goals and 18 assists in 67 games. He increased his production to 19 goals and 34 assists in 1960–61, scoring six goals in the playoffs. Mikita racked up more than 100 penalty minutes in his first two NHL seasons before settling down and earning the Lady Byng Memorial Trophy for sportsmanlike conduct twice in 1967 and 1968.

Between 1962 and 1970, Mikita consistently scored more than 30 goals per season. He led the league in assists three times and in scoring four times during his 10-year

run with the Black Hawks. He was on the January 1966 and March 1967 covers of Sports Illustrated, highlighting his huge successes with the Black Hawks.

During the latter part of his career, Mikita dealt with back injuries and retired during the 1979–80 season. At the time of his retirement, he was third in career points with 1,467, sixth in games played with 1,394, and had 541 goals.

In 1983, he was inducted into the Hockey Hall of Fame, and he joined the ranks of the 100 Greatest NHL Players in 1998. The renamed Chicago Blackhawks retired his famous number 21 jersey in 1980. As of 2022, he ranks 15th in regular season points scored in NHL history.

Mikita was an inspiration. After learning about a friend's deaf son who had NHL dreams, in 1973, Mikita founded the Stan Mikita School for the Hearing Impaired. In addition, he helped bring the Special Olympics to Chicago.

In 2011, the Chicago Blackhawks unveiled a statue of Mikita at Chicago's United Center. Mikita was fiercely proud of his Slovak origin. In 2002, he was inducted into the Slovak Hockey Hall of Fame in 2002, and he has a hockey rink in Slovakia named after him.

Mikita died on August 7, 2018, at the age of 78 after a battle with dementia. Chicago's beloved Stan Mikita was an empathetic, inspirational, and humble hockey hero.

HOWIE MORENZ

Nickname	Mitchell Meteor, Stratford Streak
Nationality	Canadian
Born	September 21, 1902
Position	Center
NHL Debut	1923-24
Teams	Montreal Canadiens, Chicago Black Hawks, New York Rangers

STANLEY CUPS
3

GOALS	ASSISTS
271	205

BIOGRAPHY

Born on September 21, 1902, in Mitchell, Ontario, Canada, 100 miles west of Toronto, Howie Morenz first learned to play hockey in the winters on the frozen Thames River. At the age of eight, he played as a goaltender but was moved to a "rover," covering any position that was needed. He was a particularly fast skater and an amazing goal scorer in the Ontario Hockey League, gaining the nickname the "Stratford Streak."

At the age of 18, Morenz worked at the Canadian National Railway (CNR) shop as an apprentice and played for the Stratford Midgets for five seasons. In one CNR tournament being played in Montreal, a game referee took notice of five-foot-nine, 165-pound Morenz and immediately advised the Montreal Canadiens that there was a future NHL star in their midst.

The Montreal Canadiens wanted to sign Morenz to a contract when he was 20, but Morenz still had two more years as a CNR apprentice. However, after there were fears from Montreal that Morenz would sign with Toronto, in 1923, the Canadiens signed him for $3,500 a year for three years with a $1,000 signing bonus.

Wearing his blue, white, and red number 7, Morenz was considered one of the NHL's first stars, winning the Stanley Cup three times with the Canadiens. He won league MVP three times and led the league in scoring twice. Morenz led Montreal in goals and points for seven consecutive seasons and finished in the top ten in scoring ten times. He won the Hart Trophy for MVP in the NHL three times in 1928, 1931, and 1932.

Morenz moved to the Chicago Black Hawks in 1934, to the New York Rangers in 1935, and then back to the Montreal Canadiens for the 1936–37 season. It was during this season that he suffered a career-ending leg injury, cutting his NHL career short after only 14 seasons.

Tragically and quite unbelievably, Morenz passed away at the age of 34 due to complications from his broken leg. Morenz had 271 goals and 205 assists in 550 career games.

The Canadiens retired his jersey number, marking the first time the team had ever done that for a player. He was one of the first nine members inducted into the Hockey Hall of Fame when it opened in 1945. In 2017, the NHL named Morenz to the list of the 100 greatest players in NHL history.

BOBBY ORR

Nickname	Number 4
Nationality	Canadian
Born	March 20, 1948
Position	Defenseman
NHL Debut	1966-67
Teams	Boston Bruins, Chicago Black Hawks

STANLEY CUPS
2

GOALS	ASSISTS
270	645

BIOGRAPHY

Hailing from Parry Sound, Ontario, Canada, Bobby Orr, one of the greatest NHL players of all time, was born on March 20, 1948. He began playing hockey at age five and started getting noticed by NHL scouts by the time he was 12.

Although the Detroit Red Wings, Montreal Canadiens, and Toronto Maple Leafs all wanted Orr, he signed with the Boston Bruins in 1962, even though he was too young to play in the NHL. He joined the Bruins' junior hockey affiliate, the Oshawa Generals, and was an all-star for three of his four seasons with the team. By this time, Orr was six feet tall and reaching 200 pounds.

In 1966, Orr joined the Bruins and scored his first assist in his first game. Four years later, they won the Stanley Cup, breaking the Bruin's 29-year cup-free streak. The Bruins won the Stanley Cup again in 1972. Orr won the Hart Memorial Trophy for league MVP in 1970, 1971, and 1972, leading the league in assists five times. He dominated in speed, scoring, and penalty-killing abilities. He could take control of the puck, rush from end to end, and make plays from the blue line. He is the only defensive player to win the Art Ross Trophy twice for leading the NHL in scoring.

In 1976, Orr left the Bruins to join the Black Hawks,

finishing his NHL career when he retired in 1978 at the age of 30. He was only able to play 26 games over three seasons with the Black Hawks due to his ongoing knee problems. He finished his career having played 657 games, scored 270 goals, and made 645 assists. Orr won a record eight straight James Norris Trophies for NHL best defenseman between 1968 and 1975 and won the MVP of the 1976 Canada Cup.

He was inducted into the Hockey Hall of Fame in 1979, the same year that the Bruins retired his number 4 jersey. In 2010, a bronze statue of Orr was unveiled next to Boston's TD Garden, showing him scoring the game-winning goal in his Stanley Cup victory. That same year, he was a flagbearer for the 2010 Winter Olympics in Vancouver. Orr released his own memoir, *Orr: My Story*, in 2013.

In 2017, Orr was named by the NHL as one of the 100 Greatest NHL Players in History.

ALEX OVECHKIN

Nickname	Ovi, Alexander the GR8
Nationality	Russian
Born	September 17, 1985
Position	Left Wing
NHL Debut	2005-06
Teams	Washington Capitals

STANLEY CUPS

1

GOALS	ASSISTS
780	630

BIOGRAPHY

Alex "Ovi" Ovechkin was born in Moscow on September 17, 1985. Ovechkin picked up a hockey stick for the first time at the age of two and studied televised NHL games, especially those of his favorite team, the San Jose Sharks. He attended a strict Russian public school for eight and a half grades before starting at Dynamo Moscow, a sports school.

Ovechkin began his professional career with the Dynamo Moscow of the Russian Super League in 2001 when he was 16. He represented Russia at the 2002 World U18 Championship and the following year made his first appearance at the World Junior Championship, winning a gold medal with team Russia.

In the 2004 NHL Draft, the Washington Capitals selected Ovechkin as first pick, but he'd remain in the Russia Super League throughout the 2004–05 hockey season because of the NHL lockout. He would finally play his first game with the Capitals in October of 2005. He would become known for "The Goal" in a game against the Phoenix Coyotes in January 2006. He had fallen onto his back but still managed to hook the puck with only one hand on his stick and miraculously score. Ovechkin won the Calder Memorial Trophy for the league's best rookie after recording 52 goals and 54 assists. By 2007–08, he'd sign a 13-year deal with the Capitals, but he'd

have to wait until 2018 for his first Stanley Cup with them.

Ovechkin quickly became one of the superstars of the NHL, winning the Hart Memorial Trophy for MVP in 2008, 2009, and 2013. A dominant goal scorer, Ovechkin has led the league in scoring nine times between 2008 and 2020, taking home the Maurice Richard Trophy. He has scored 50 goals in a season a remarkable nine times.

Ovechkin also played for Russia in the Winter Olympics in 2006, where he scored five goals in eight games. He played for Russia again in 2010 and 2014. He was named one of the 100 Greatest NHL Players of all time in 2017.

Entering the 2022–23 season, Ovechkin has 780 goals and 630 assists in 1,274 games. He wants to close out his NHL career with the Capitals but has publicly declared his wish for his last hockey game to be with the Dynamo Moscow.

Ovechkin has been giving back to the community since 2006 through his Ovi's Crazy 8 charity. He gives away eight home-game seats to children in need, soldiers, and their families. They are treated to special seats in the Verizon Center. He is a genuine guy and a hockey legend.

DENIS POTVIN

Nickname	Unknown
Nationality	Canadian
Born	October 29, 1953
Position	Defenseman
NHL Debut	1973-74
Teams	New York Islanders

STANLEY CUPS
4

GOALS	ASSISTS
310	742

BIOGRAPHY

Denis Potvin was born on October 29, 1953, in Ottawa, Ontario, Canada but grew up in Hull, Quebec. Like so many other Canadian NHL players we've already covered, he got his hockey start playing on his backyard rink. He loved to watch the Montreal Canadiens. He spent his junior hockey time with the Ottawa 67s and was drafted first overall in the 1973 Draft by the New York Islanders, who were coming off the worst record in league history.

Potvin had a lot of pressure on him as a rookie for the Islanders, as many people were likening him to Bobby Orr. He didn't disappoint as right out of the gate, Potvin won the Calder Memorial Trophy as the league's top rookie in 1973–74, scoring 54 points in 77 games. He won the James Norris Memorial Trophy as NHL best defenseman in 1975–76. At just 22 years old, Potvin scored 98 points and surpassed the 100-point mark in 1978–79, becoming the second defenseman after Orr to reach that plateau.

He enjoyed his best scoring years in 1975–76 and again in 1978–79, with 31 goals in each. Potvin was named captain of the team in the 1979–80 season. That same year, he won his first of four Stanley Cups with the Islanders. He made history as being the first NHL player to reach 100 assists in playoffs and the first defenseman

to reach 300 goals during regular season play. He loved physical and defensive hockey and was a natural leader.

In the eight seasons that Potvin was captain, the Islanders made the playoffs each year. After multiple injuries over the next few years, Potvin retired following the 1987–88 season with 310 goals and 742 assists over 1,060 games played.

His jersey, number 5, was retired by the Islanders in 1992, a first for the franchise. As of 2022, he remains one of only two players to have played more than 1,000 games for the Islanders. At the end of his career, just as people had predicted at the start of it, he had broken all the goal and point records set by Bobby Orr!

After his retirement, he entered the broadcasting world, where he stayed until 2019. Potvin joined the Hockey Hall of Fame in 1991, and in 2017, he was named one of the 100 Greatest NHL Players in History.

MAURICE RICHARD

Nickname	The Comet, The Rocket
Nationality	Canadian
Born	August 4, 1921
Position	Right wing
NHL Debut	1942-43
Teams	Montreal Canadiens

STANLEY CUPS
8

GOALS	ASSISTS
544	422

BIOGRAPHY

Maurice, the "Rocket," Richard was born on August 4, 1921, in Montreal, Quebec, Canada, and was the oldest of eight kids in his family. He started skating at the age of four on local rivers and a small backyard ice surface. His family struggled through the Great Depression. Money was tight, so his first opportunity to play organized hockey didn't happen until he was 14. By age 17, he had already led his team to three consecutive championships and scored 133 of the team's 144 goals.

Richard dropped out of school at the age of 16 to work as a machinist to help the family out financially. At the age of 18, Richard became a member of the Verdun A Junior Maple Leafs in Montreal, but his job took up most of his time, and he only played ten games. In 1940, Richard was picked up by the Montreal Senior Canadiens in the Quebec Senior Hockey League (the Canadien's farm team) but missed the season with a broken ankle.

Richard would make his NHL debut with the Canadiens in the 1942–43 season. He had a short temper, which led to many NHL fights, much to the delight of his fans. One of his suspensions led to fans engaging outside the Montreal Forum in one of the worst riots in Canada's sports history.

Richard worked well under pressure and had incredible

speed, which angered opposition teams who fought back with all kinds of slashing and hooking. His quick skating abilities were what led to him being called the "Rocket" and the "Comet." He was part of eight Stanley Cup championship teams that included a record five straight from 1956 to 1960.

He was the first NHL player to reach 50 goals in a game, accomplishing the feat in the 1944–45 season in just 50 games. Richard won the Hart Memorial Trophy as the NHL's MVP in 1947. He was also the first to score 500 career goals and retired in 1960 with 544 goals and 422 assists in 978 games over 18 seasons.

After spending his whole career with the Canadiens, the team retired Richard's number 9 shortly after his retirement in 1960. The Hall of Fame waived its five-year waiting period for eligibility and inducted Richard into the Hockey Hall of Fame in 1961. In 1975, Richard was inducted into Canada's Sports Hall of Fame, and in 1999, the NHL began the Maurice "Rocket" Richard Trophy, which is awarded annually to the league's regular season leader in goals.

Richard passed away on May 27, 2000, and he was named one of the 100 Greatest NHL Players in History in 2017. He was a true hockey hero who earned his way through the NHL ranks.

PATRICK ROY

Nickname	Saint Patrick
Nationality	Canadian
Born	October 5, 1965
Position	Goalie
NHL Debut	1984–85
Teams	Montreal Canadiens, Colorado Avalanche

STANLEY CUPS
4

CAREER WINS	GOALS AGAINST AVERAGE
551	2.54

BIOGRAPHY

Born on October 5, 1965 in Quebec City, Quebec, Canada, Patrick Roy grew up in Cap-Rouge, Quebec. He started playing hockey at the age of seven, and he knew immediately that he wanted to be a goalie. He played in both the Quebec Major Junior Hockey and the American Hockey Leagues. In the 1984 NHL Entry Draft, Roy was selected by the Montreal Canadiens.

He'd have a chance to play his first game as a goalie for the NHL on February 23, 1985. He'd be sent to the American Hockey League for the remainder of that season so he could learn more about how hockey was played in the pro leagues. By the next season in 1985–86, Roy would play his rookie year with the Canadiens and the team would win their first Stanley Cup with him in goal. He won the Conn Smthye trophy that year for the most outstanding playoff player and gained his new nickname, "Saint Patrick."

Roy moved to the Colorado Avalanche in the 1995–96 season, where he would remain until he retired after the 2002–03 season. He'd win two more Stanley Cups over his time with the Avalanche. Over his career, he won three Vezina trophies, awarded by the NHL for the best goalie. He was the first NHL goaltender to cross the 1,000 games played threshold.

Roy retired with 551 wins, 66 shutouts, and 28,346 shots fired against him while in net. He finished with 2.54 goals against average and a .910 save percentage. It seems that his game-day superstitions paid off for him. He'd always speak to the goalposts before his games and would never step directly on the red or blue lines on the ice.

Both the Canadiens and the Avalanche retired his number 33 jersey. Roy led the league in save percentage four times and in goals against average and shutouts two times.

After retiring as a player, Roy became owner, general manager, and head coach of the Quebec Remparts in the Quebec Major Junior Hockey League. He led the Remparts to the 2006 Memorial Cup, winning the QMJHL championship. In 2013, Roy became head coach and vice-president of operations of the Colorado Avalanche before stepping down in 2016.

Roy was named into the Hockey Hall of Fame in 2006 and as one of the 100 Greatest NHL Players in History in 2017.

TERRY SAWCHUK

Nickname	Ukie
Nationality	Canadian
Born	December 28, 1929
Position	Goalie
NHL Debut	1949–50
Teams	Detroit Red Wings, Boston Bruins, Toronto Maple Leafs, Los Angeles Kings, New York Rangers

STANLEY CUPS
4

CAREER WINS
445

SHUTOUTS
103

Terry "Ukie" Sawchuk was born on December 28, 1929, in Winnipeg, Manitoba, Canada. At the age of 12, Sawchuk injured his right elbow playing rugby but hid the injury, which prevented it from healing properly. His right arm ended up being almost six inches shorter than his left.

Sawchuk started playing ice hockey in a local league. He inherited his first goalie pads from his brother, who had tragically passed away from a heart attack as a teen. Sawchuk displayed considerable talent as a goaltender by the age of 14 and got noticed by a Detroit Red Wings scout. He initially joined the Red Wings farm team in the US Hockey League. By 1947, when he was just 18, he had signed his first NHL professional contract with them.

Sawchuk continued to impress, leading the Red Wings to the Stanley Cup in the 1949–50 season and followed by his first Calder Trophy as the NHL's top rookie in 1950–51. In his career, he won a total of four Stanley Cups, three with the Detroit Red Wings and one with the Boston Bruins.

He suffered an incredible number of excruciating injuries, which included more than 400 stitches and ruptured discs in his back from always being hunched over. He didn't even wear a goalie mask until 1962!

Sawchuk always tried to hide his pain, but it likely is why his teammates described him as miserable and angry a lot of the time.

After five full seasons with Detroit, he was traded to the Bruins in 1955, where he'd play a partial season with them in 1956–57 before heading back to Detroit until the end of the 1963–64 season. He bounced from the Toronto Maple Leafs to the Los Angeles Kings, back to Detroit, then finished off with the New York Rangers, for 21 total seasons in the NHL. In regular season play, he recorded 445 wins and 103 shutouts with 2.50 goals against average. He won the Vezina Trophy for the top goalie in the NHL four times.

He was the all-time leader in wins and shutouts at the time of his death, and his win total has been surpassed by only five other goals more than 50 years after his death. Sawchuk died quite unexpectedly on May 31, 1970, when he was only 40 years old. He was elected to the Hockey Hall of Fame the year after his final season.

In 2017, Sawchuk was named one of the 100 Greatest NHL Players of all time. He obviously had true grit and sheer determination.

EDDIE SHORE

Nickname	Edmonton Express
Nationality	Canadian
Born	November 25, 1902
Position	Defenseman
NHL Debut	1926–27
Teams	Boston Bruins, New York Americans

STANLEY CUPS

2

GOALS	ASSISTS
105	179

BIOGRAPHY

Eddie Shore, a dominant defenseman in the NHL, was born on November 25, 1902, in Fort Qu'Appelle, Saskatchewan, Canada. He started his minor hockey journey with Cupar Canucks before he moved up to the professionals with the Western Canada Hockey League in 1925, suiting up for the Regina Capitals. Shore moved to the Edmonton Eskimos in 1926, gaining his nickname "the Edmonton Express" when he made the switch from forward to defenseman, where he dominated for the rest of his NHL career.

The Western Hockey League folded in 1926, paving Shore's way to the NHL and the Boston Bruins. Shore was more of a bruiser than anything else during his rookie season, scoring 18 points and 130 penalty minutes. He was the Bruin's tough guy who didn't shy away from on-ice confrontations, leading the league in penalty minutes with 165 in his second season. He was on the 1929 Bruins team when they secured the Stanley Cup.

In 1933, Shore was involved in an on-ice crash that sent Toronto Maple Leaf's right-winger Ace Bailey into the boards, knocking him out. Bailey would spend ten days in a coma and never play for the NHL again. Shore would be suspended for 16 games after that incident.

Shore combined both speed and excellent stick handling

to become a fan favorite. He was just what the NHL needed to secure their success as they expanded into the US. He won the Hart Trophy for league MVP four times, the most by any defenseman in NHL history. After the Bruins won their 1939 Stanley Cup, he was briefly traded to the New York Americans before he retired from the NHL, clocking 550 games with 105 goals.

Next, Shore went on to buy and play for the Springfield Indians in the American Hockey League for two seasons. After halting their play for two seasons due to World War II, the Indians resumed playing in 1946, and Shore returned to the team.

Shore joined the Hockey Hall of Fame in 1947, the same year Boston retired his number 2 jersey. He was named one of the 100 Greatest NHL Players in History in 2017. Shore passed away of liver cancer on March 16, 1985, at the age of 82. He was furiously competitive, tough as nails, and adored by his fans.

STEVE YZERMAN

Nickname	Stevie Y, The Captain, Stevie Wonder
Nationality	Canadian
Born	May 9, 1965
Position	Center
NHL Debut	1983-84
Teams	Detroit Red Wings

STANLEY CUPS
3

GOALS	ASSISTS
692	1063

BIOGRAPHY

Steve Yzerman, a Detroit sports icon, was born on May 9, 1965, in Cranbrook, British Columbia, Canada. Yzerman really had to work on his skating skills when he first started playing organized hockey in his hometown.

His family moved to Ontario, just outside of Ottawa, when he was ten, and his hockey career really took off. As an amateur, he first played with the Nepean Raiders in the Central Junior Hockey League and was then drafted by the Peterborough Petes of the Ontario Hockey League.

Once he turned 18, he was selected by the Detroit Red Wings 4th overall in the 1983 NHL Draft. The Detroit team was struggling. Many people in that city called them "The Dead Things," and Yzerman was just what they needed to light a spark.

He made the All-Rookie team and finished second in Calder Cup voting for rookie of the year after scoring 87 points in 80 games in his first year. He was derailed by a broken collarbone for much of the 1985–86 season but came back with force and gained the title of team captain in the next season.

At 21, Yzerman was the youngest captain ever to be named in the NHL at the time. He'd remain captain of the Red Wings for the duration of his 22-year career.

Yzerman was once voted the most popular athlete in the history of Detroit sports. It's no wonder. Between 1987 and 1993, Yzerman would score more than 100 points each season. In 1993, he was dealt another major health blow when a hit from behind caused him to need major back surgery. He never let an injury take him down, though. After fourteen hard-fought years of skating with the Red Wings, he led them to the Stanley Cup in 1997 and achieved his childhood dream.

Yzerman led the team to three Stanley Cup Championships. He scored at least 30 goals in a season 11 times, over 50 goals four times, and had a season-high of 65 in 1988–89.

Yzerman was the recipient of many awards during his career, including the Lester B. Pearson Award for most outstanding player in 1988-89, the Conn Smythe Trophy for MVP of the playoffs in 1998, and the Selke Trophy for the league's best defensive forward in 2000. He played in ten All-Star games and retired in 2006 with 692 goals and 1,063 assists. Yzerman's famous number 19 jersey was retired in 2007. He was inducted into the Hockey Hall of Fame in 2009.

In 2017, Yzerman was named one of the 100 Greatest NHL Players in History. He was an incredibly classy leader who was humble. He cared more about his team's overall performance than his own personal stats, and he showed it every time he stepped on the ice.